Know Your Ducks

Jack Byard

Old Pond Publishing

First published 2011

Copyright © Jack Byard, 2011

The moral rights of the author in this work have been asserted.

ISBN 978-1-906853-82-2

Published by
Old Pond Publishing Ltd
Dencora Business Centre
36 White House Road
Ipswich IP1 5LT
United Kingdom

www.oldpond.com

Book design by Liz Whatling
Printed and bound in China

Contents

Acknowledgments

Many thanks to all the enthusiasts and breeders who have kindly supplied me with information and photographs; without their help this project could not have taken to the water. I am also most grateful to all these people for taking time in their busy schedules to answer my questions with what, to them, is fairly basic knowledge.

And once again thanks to Rebecca whose 'old fashioned' looks keep grandad on the straight and narrow.

Any mistakes are mine and mine alone.

Picture Credits

(1) Tim Daniels of www.poultrykeeper.com, (2) Morag Jones, (3) Ancona ducks at ISeeSpots Farm courtesy of Mary Ellen Hansson, (4) Dave Holderread at Holderread Waterfowl Farm and Preservation Centre, (5) Debbie Kingsley, (6) Morag Jones, (7) Debbie Hillman of Ark Birds and Bees, Kent, (8) Mark Wagoner – Goldendale, Washington USA, (9) David Brandreth, (10) Morag Jones, (11) Linda Dick, (12) Carole Bryant, (13) Mark Wagoner – Goldendale, Washington USA, (14) David Brandreth, (15) Moon Ridge Farm, (16) Trevor Jarrold, 17) Mark Wagoner – Goldendale, Washington USA, (18) Moon Ridge Farm, (19) Moon Ridge Farm, (20) Trevor Jarrold, (21) David Brandreth, (22) Dave Holderread at Holderread Waterfowl Farm and Preservation Centre, (23) Christopher Gunn, (24) Mark Wagoner – Goldendale, Washington USA, (25) Moon Ridge Farm, (26) David Brandreth, (27) David Brandreth, (28) Mark Wagoner – Goldendale, Washington USA, (29) Moon Ridge Farm, (30) David Brandreth, (31) Mark Wagoner – Goldendale, Washington USA, (32) Mark Wagoner – Goldendale, Washington USA, (33) Vince Smith, (34) Triple Spring Acres, (35) Mark Wagoner – Goldendale, Washington USA, (36) Dave Holderread at Holderread Waterfowl Farm and Preservation Centre, (37) David Brandreth, (38) Dave Holderread at Holderread Waterfowl Farm and Preservation Centre, (39) Angela L Ryniak, www.naturesaddition.com, (40) David Brandreth, (41) Anders Gustavsson, (42) Lee Karney, (43) Dave Holderread at Holderread Waterfowl Farm and Preservation Centre, (44) David Brandreth.

Foreword

I think most of us can remember, in our childhood, visiting the local pond or stretch of canal to feed the ducks and anything that remotely resembled a duck; throwing breadcrumbs in the water and in a matter of seconds being confronted with a hoard of quacking, flapping waterfowl as a mixture of joy and panic fills your heart.

It never fails to amaze me to watch the tiny ball-of-fluff ducklings which have been hatched in a tree nest throwing themselves the many metres to the ground where mum is urging them on. They hit the ground, bounce and with a quick shake of the feathers they follow mum. Don't try this at home.

Sadly, a number of duck breeds are now under extreme threat of extinction. There have always been natural predators but now a major problem in some parts of the world is that their breeding areas are being reduced or destroyed.

In my other *Know Your...* books I have tried to indicate where each breed can be found today. In the case of ducks which can fly immense distances, it is a little more difficult to say. A number of the ducks mentioned in this book are not classed as official residents of the British Isles but all have been spotted here in various numbers. Some have arrived courtesy of a tail wind to visit or stay while others have absconded from private collections to live in the wild.

JACK BYARD
2010

1.

Abacot Ranger

Native to
The British Isles

Description

The Abacot Ranger was developed by Oscar Gray of the Abacot Duck Ranch near Colchester. They are a cross between a khaki Campbell and a white Indian Runner and all the breeding and development took place between 1917 and 1923. In 1925 the Abacot Ranger disappeared from the British landscape but fortunately they had arrived in Germany via Denmark in 1926 where the breed was further improved and standardised. It was re-discovered in the British Isles in the 1980s.

In an egg-laying test at Wye College in 1922 and 1923, four Abacot Rangers laid 935 eggs in a year. That's a good number by any standard. For an Abacot Ranger kept in your garden a more likely number is 180 to 200 white eggs per year.

They are a good all-round breed with the added bonus of flying like a brick. Given safe, warm housing they can live for up to fourteen years although, once they reach ten, extra care must be taken in the winter as they become waterlogged.

Colour

The male's under-body is creamy-white. The back has white-fringed black dots which become bigger until they meet the rump which is green-tinted black. The breast and shoulder feathers are claret edged with white. The head and neck are greenish-black. The bill is usually green with a black tip and the legs and feet are orange. The female is cream with light brown streaks and a hood of fawn feathers. Her bill, legs and feet are dark grey.

2.

African Yellow Billed

Native to
Africa

Description

This African freshwater duck does not migrate. Instead, in the dry season it becomes a nomad, wandering the open countryside of southern and eastern Africa in search of suitable fresh water such as lakes, rivers, marshes and slow-flowing estuaries. Outside the breeding season they congregate in massive flocks of several thousand. The male has to work hard to impress the female with preening, synchronised swimming, acrobatic flying, strange noises and fighting off rivals. In the breeding season the Yellow Billed male is a one-girl guy and will only choose another mate if his partner dies.

The female builds her nest in a hollow in the ground and lines it with vegetation. It is never far from water. The clutch consists of four to twelve creamy-yellow or buff coloured eggs which are laid at one per day.

The African Yellow Billed's typical diet consists of grass, crickets and grasshoppers, grain and seeds. Apart from natural predators they are hunted for use in traditional medicines and are being greatly affected by pollution.

Colour

The male and female are almost identical. The body is dark brown and the feathers have buff coloured edges. Some of the wing feathers are iridescent green with white tips. The head and neck are dark grey with pale streaks. The male's bill is yellow with a central black stripe and a black tip, the female's is not as bright. The eyes are brown and the legs and feet vary between yellow, reddish-brown and greyish-black.

3.

Ancona

Black and White

Native to
The British Isles

Description

The Ancona is a rare British duck which was developed in the 20th century by crossing the Indian Runner with the Belgian Huttengem. It has an unusual mottled appearance and is made up of two or, on occasion, three colours; this random patterning is also visible on the bill, feet and legs. No two ducks have the same pattern.

A good dual-purpose breed, this calm and friendly duck will make a good pet and is ideal for the smallholding or garden. If allowed to roam it will forage for some of its food and help keep your patch clear of slugs. This home-loving bird does not tend to wander although, like most ducks, they need to be locked away at night to protect them from the local dogs and foxes.

The Ancona was first seen in America at an exhibition in Oregon in 1983 and became available to the general public a year later. Although the numbers are increasing it is listed as 'critical' in the USA.

Colour

They are white with random patches of another colour all over. Combinations include black and white, chocolate and white, blue and white, silver and white and lavender and white. The bill is yellow with black or green spots and the feet and legs are orange with random black markings that increase with age.

4.

Australian Spotted

Silverheaded

Native to
America

The Australian Spotted, despite its name, is not from Australia. This American breed was developed in Pennsylvania by John C Kriner Jnr. and Stanley Mason in 1920. It is a cross between the Mallard, the Pintail and the Call duck as well as an unidentified species of Australian wild duck that was persuaded to stay for a while. The four breeds were housed together and allowed to interbreed until, through careful selection and over many generations, this beautiful but rare species was created.

The Australian Spotted is an excellent mother and lays in the region of 50-125 cream, green or blue eggs a year. This hardy and long-lived duck is ideal if you have too many slugs and snails and will sort the problem out. If your garden is small you will need to clip their wings or you will soon need to buy replacement ducks.

Males have a silver head and a white band around the neck. The neck is fawn and spotted with brown. The body and sides are deep burgundy and the breast and under-body are white. The back is dark grey and the wings are a dark greyish-brown. The tail is light grey and black. The bill is greenish-yellow, the eyes are brown and the legs and feet are orange. The female is shades of buff and creamy-brown. Other colours are greenheaded and blueheaded.

5.

Aylesbury

Native to
The British Isles

Description

The Aylesbury has a horizontal stance with its body parallel to the ground, though not all white ducks with a horizontal gait are Aylesburys. This is a breed dating back to the 18th century and to find a true purebred example is very rare. Breeding these ducks was once a cottage industry in and around Aylesbury in Buckinghamshire where was raised for food. In cold weather the ducks would be kept inside the cottage and since hygiene standards were next to nil the smell would have been overpowering. The ducks would have been walked the 40 or so miles to the London market to be sold to the rich. To protect the birds' feet they were walked through a cold tar solution and then through sawdust; the result, duck boots.

The Aylesbury duck lays in the region of 35 to 125 large white eggs a year. A slight difference in breeding or diet means that in America the eggs are blue. They are not often seen in flight, like a Jumbo jet they need a long runway. In the mid 19th century duck breeding in the Aylesbury area, for many reasons, started to decline.

Any colour as long as it is white. The bill is pale pink and the legs and feet are bright orange.

6.

Baikal Teal

Native to
Central and eastern Siberia

Description

This bright and attractive bird is classed as a dabbling duck meaning it feeds by dipping its head and upending its body in the water. Its flamboyant appearance makes it stand out from other dabbling ducks.

Most Baikal Teals winter in southern Siberia, Mongolia, Korea, eastern China, Japan and occasionally Alaska. The breed was once one of the most numerous in Asia but in the mid 20th century numbers dropped dramatically, causing great concern. The main cause was over-hunting, loss of habitat and farmers protecting their rice crops. Lately numbers have been improving but I have been told that one of the main wintering areas in South Korea is to be developed for tourism, posing another threat to the breed.

The female Baikal Teal builds her nest on dry ground concealed by grass and shrubs, always within waddling distance of water. She lays between six and nine pale green eggs and the male leaves before they hatch. These ducks have a diet of leaves, grasses and the occasional snail.

Colour

The male's upper-body has long cinnamon, cream and black feathers. The under-body is white, the breast is pink and buff with black spots and the sides are grey with vertical white lines. The head has dark brown, buff and green patches trimmed by white and black. The wings are dark brown and grey. The legs, feet and bill are grey and the eyes are brown. The female is brown with a white spot just behind her bill.

7.

Bali

Native to
Bali

Description

The Bali is an ancient breed known in its homeland for over 2,000 years which makes it one of the oldest domestic breeds of duck. It is thought by a number of experts to be an ancestor of the Indian Runner duck and it is similar to them in appearance: a bowling pin with legs. The main differences are that the Bali has shoulders and a crest the size of a golf ball on the back of the head. While white is the most common colour of the Bali in the western world, brown is most commonly seen in the east.

The Bali does not have a huge following outside Bali and Malaysia and it has a high mortality rate so is not an easy duck to breed. It was re-introduced into the British Isles in the 1990s by crossing a Bali with an Indian Runner and I am told this cross has improved the survival rate. The Bali is bred mainly as a decorative duck and lays between 100 and 200 blue-green to white eggs a year.

They are white. The legs and feet are orange, the bill is an orange-yellow and the eyes are blue.

Black-Bellied Whistling

Native to
America

Description

Many bird enthusiasts travel to Texas just to see the Black-Bellied Whistling duck which is a year-long resident on the Texas Gulf Coast. It thrives on coastal wetlands, marshes and shallow lagoons where it lives on a mainly vegetarian diet. The calm and gentle nature of the bird has, in the past, made it an easy target for hunters. Current hunting, so I understand, is usually to prevent large groups landing on a field full of tender juicy shoots.

The Black-Bellied Whistling was originally known as the Black-Bellied Tree duck for its habit of building its nest in holes in tree trunks (although it sometimes chooses a bed of reeds at ground level). A clutch of eggs is usually twelve to sixteen whitish eggs laid at one per day and the eggs and the ducklings are cared for by both parents. It is thought they pair for life. Because of their docile temperament they are content in captivity with other species of waterfowl. Their call is a screeching *pee-chee*.

Colour

The male and female birds are similar in size and colour. The body, back of the neck and top of the head are rich chestnut brown and the under-body, tail and rump are black. The wings are dark brown with a large white patch. The upper neck and face are grey with white spectacles. The bill is bright red, the long legs are pink and the eyes are dark brown.

9.

Black East Indian

Native to
America

Description

The Black East Indian is the oldest bantam duck breed and, here's a surprise, it has nothing to do with the East Indies. The name was more than likely an advertising gimmick. It is also known as Le Canard Labrador, the Buenos Aires and the Black Brazilian. Its true place of origin is unknown but America has been put on its birth certificate.

The Black East Indian is not the best of layers, only producing a clutch of 10 to 20 eggs each season. Those laid early in the season are black to dark grey but those laid later in the season will be light grey or blue. These ducks are best kept in pairs or trios.

The Black East Indian has always been described as an eye-catching bird. In 1943 three professional artists were asked to select the most beautiful bird from 5,000 and chose the Black East Indian.

Bronze Winged

Native to
South America

Description

The Bronze Winged duck, also known as the Spectacled, lives in the forested areas of South America, on the lower slopes of the Andes and in the magnificent Argentinian region of Tierra del Fuego. They live by the mountain streams, rivers, and lakes where they feed off small fish, snails, crabs and vegetation.

The Bronze Winged duck is normally a calm and easy-going bird but can become aggressive in the breeding season and has been known to kill much larger birds. Pairs bond for long periods. They build their nests on the ground in dense vegetation and line them with down. The clutch normally consists of four to six creamy-coloured eggs and after they hatch both parents look after the brood.

With an estimated population of 10,000, the Bronze Winged is classed as 'near threatened' by the IUCN (the International Union for Conservation of Nature). The biggest threats to their existence are the American mink, salmon farming, trout stocking on Chilean rivers and increased tourism.

Colour

The head, upper-neck and upper-body are dark brown, sometimes with a buff tint. There are white patches on the face and side of the neck. The under-body, lower-neck and breast are a dull brown with buff-edged feathers. The wings are a dark brown to purplish-black with some white-tipped feathers. The bill is dark grey with a black tip, the eyes are brown and the legs and feet are yellow-orange. The males and females look largely alike.

11.

Call
White

Native to
Probably the Far East

Description

Historically the Call duck was used as a decoy, possibly in Holland as far back as the 17th century. Some experts believe that the Coy or De Koot, as it was known, could have been used even before this.

When working as a decoy, a tame Call duck would be tethered (usually a female because she quacks louder than the male) and whilst it paddled across the lake the handler would pull on the tether. The duck, thinking it was being attacked, would quack. Passing ducks would fly in to investigate and they would be shot for the commercial meat market. It would appear that breeding the Call for meat has never been financially viable. It was also thought they looked so beautiful on the water it would be 'proper' to leave them there.

This noisy duck is full of character so not a good choice if you have peace-loving neighbours. They lay between 25 and 75 bluish-green eggs a year.

Colour

They are pure white. The bill is yellow, the legs and feet are bright orange, and the eyes are blue. Other colours include: grey; blue; buff; pastel; khaki; butterscotch; chocolate; snowy; spot and black.

Campbell
Khaki

Native to
The British Isles

Description

Trying to trace the ancestry of many ducks is often similar to walking in a maze, you are always uncertain about your position. The Campbell is refreshingly different. In the 19th century Adele Campbell of Uley in Gloucestershire decided she wanted a breed that would give her white eggs for breakfast but which, when perfected, would not simply disappear into the wide blue yonder. She crossed a fawn and white Indian Runner with a Rouen to produce a good layer with a larger body. The results of this cross were, in turn, crossed with a Mallard to increase their strength and disease resistance. In 1898 the Campbell was unveiled to the public. To further improve the appearance of the Campbell one more cross was carried out, this time with a penciled Indian Runner, and result was the khaki Campbell so named because it reminded Mrs Campbell of the British Army uniforms.

The khaki Campbell lays between 200 and 300 eggs a year. In 1901 it was accepted as a UK standard.

Colour

The main body colour is a bronze-brown, khaki. The head, neck, rump and wing bar are a greenish-bronze, the bill is dark green and the legs and feet are orange. The female is slightly darker on the back and the wings. Her legs and feet are khaki. Other colours include: blue; apricot; white and dark.

13.

Carolina

Native to
America and Mexico

Description

The Carolina is found in large numbers in North American woodlands close to water, ranging from Hudson Bay through to Mexico and the Caribbean. These beautiful, elegant birds with their rich plumage are universally popular in waterfowl collections. A flock of Carolina ducks is recorded in Surrey. However, they are not thought to be a viable self-sustaining group but rather a group of escapees or vagrants.

Carolinas nest in tall trees and lay their nine to fourteen white to brownish-white eggs in holes in the trunk. The newly hatched ducklings jump as much as 7 metres to the ground and walk away uninjured to the nearest water.

In the early 20th century Carolina numbers were in rapid decline due to loss of habitat and commercial hunting for meat and feathers. The feathers were exported to Europe for use in millinery (hat making). Commercial hunting has since been banned and sports hunting regulated so numbers have dramatically increased. Many landowners now encourage the Carolina by building nest boxes.

Colour

The male has a green, purple and black head with white lines and purple and green wings with a white band at the front. The under-body and throat are white, the breast is chestnut with white spots and the eyes are red with orange surrounds. The bill is red and black. The female has a grey head with white lines. The upper-body and breast are olive-brown with white spots. The bill and feet are grey.

14.

Cayuga

Native to
America

The Cayuga is named after a lake in New York state. In the mid 19th century, so the story goes, a passing miller grabbed a couple of wild black ducks and, by means not specified, kept them on his local pond. Today's Cayuga is a descendant of these ducks crossed with the Black East Indian to improve its appearance. To see their feathers glowing in bright sunlight is a sight to behold. The Cayuga can live for up to twelve years and tends to go white with age.

Apart from their exquisite appearance they are in great demand for their meat and eggs. The hen will lay between 80 and 100 eggs each season; at the beginning of the season they are black to dark grey then fade to sky blue as the season progresses.

This is a gentle, quiet bird with a quack that will not annoy the neighbours so it makes an ideal pet which will keep your garden free of slugs, snails and other nasties. The American Livestock Breeds Conservancy lists the Cayuga as endangered.

Colour

They are black beetle-green with a black bill, legs and feet and dark brown eyes.

Chiloe Wigeon

Native to
South America

Description

The Chiloe Wigeon is one of just three species of wigeon and is closely related to the Gadwall duck. It is named after Chiloe Island off the coast of Chile and can be found on the Falkland Islands and in small numbers as a summer visitor to the British Isles.

The Chiloe is to be found near the lagoons, freshwater lakes, rivers and marshes of South America where it will nest amongst the tall vegetation laying clutches of five to eight white or pale fawn eggs. The male will not assist in incubating the eggs but will guard the nest and when the ducklings are hatched he will help in rearing them. If the female does not return to the nest he will continue to do so.

The Chiloe is an ideal duck for the urban keeper; no loud quacking to annoy the neighbours and provided you have plenty of vegetation and sufficient water in which to dabble, you will have a colourful companion for up to twenty years.

The male has a green-and-black head with white cheeks and forehead. The breast is barred white and the sides are orange-brown. The back is dark grey with white streaks and there is white on the wings and rump. The tail is black. The bill is blue-grey with a black tip, the eyes are brown and the feet and legs are dark grey. The female is almost identical but not as bright.

Eider

Native to
The coasts of Northern Europe, the British Isles, North America and Eastern Siberia

Description

The Eider is a sea duck and the largest duck in the northern hemisphere, weighing in at an average of 2.5kg. The down of the Eider was traditionally used to make bedding, in particular the aptly named eiderdown. The down is remarkably warm and a sleeping bag filled with eider down and weighing only 1.5kg will keep you protected to minus 35°C. There are many scare stories about the collection of the down but ethical manufacturers collect it from the nests on Eider farms in Iceland and Scandinavia once the ducks have flown.

The Eider lays up to eight eggs which are a pale olive-green. She lays one per day and after the second egg is laid will pull down from her breast to line the nest. To protect her eggs from gulls and foxes the female will not feed during the 28 days of incubation and lives entirely off her fat reserves. Once the eggs hatch the females form crèches of up to 100 ducklings which are guarded by all the females including non-breeding aunties. Their call is a gentle *ah-ooo*.

Colour

The male has a short thick neck which is green at the top. The top of the head is black with a narrow white parting. The upper-body, chin, throat, neck and cheeks are white and the breast is buff-pink. The tail is black. The legs and triangular bill are olive-green and the eyes are brown. The female is a dark to rusty brown with an olive-grey to olive-yellow bill. The legs are grey-green.

17.

Gadwall

Native to
The British Isles, Northern Europe, North America and Asia

Description

The Gadwall was first mentioned by Carl Linnaeus, one of the fathers of modern ecology. In 1758 he gave the Gadwall its scientific name but there is fossil evidence to suggest the breed itself goes back 125,000 years.

Though they are not seen in large numbers in the British Isles, you will have the best chance in winter when the resident population is increased by visitors from around 800 pairs to a staggering 17,000 individuals. The increasing world population is estimated at an amazing 2.8 million. There are even two breeding pairs in the grounds of Buckingham Palace. They tend to gather at the edges of lakes, reservoirs and coastal wetlands as long as there is plenty of vegetation.

The nest, built on the ground near water, is made of grass and weeds lined with down. The clutch is usually eight to twelve creamy-white or pale pink eggs. The female call is described as *gag-ag-ag-ag* and the male as *nheck* and a whistle. The mind boggles.

The male is speckled grey with a black tail and rump, bright white inner wing feathers and a dark grey bill. The female is light brown with white under-body and inner wing feathers and a bright orange edge to the bill. Both have brown eyes and orange-yellow legs.

18.

Garganey

Native to
Western Europe
and Western Asia

Description

The Garganey is another duck of ancient lineage which fossil evidence proves was around 500,000 years ago. The name is derived from a 16th century Italian dialect and in 1758 it was mentioned by ecologist Carl Linnaeus in his book *Systema Naturae*. In the Camargue region of France it is known as the Cacherel and the designer Jean Bousquet was so inspired by the duck he named one of his popular fragrances after them.

About 130 pairs of Garganeys arrive in the British Isles in the spring. The ducks have already paired off before arriving from West Africa where they winter in flocks of up to 200,000 birds. They can fly at up to 60 mph.

Their preferred nesting areas are shallow freshwater lakes, reed beds and wet meadows where the banks are heavily fringed with vegetation. The nests are built on the ground amongst this vegetation and lined with feathers and down. They lay between six and fourteen pale-straw to light-brown eggs.

The male has a grey upper-body with black streaks, mottled brown face and breast, pale grey mottled sides and a white stripe over the eye and down the neck. The shoulder feathers are striped with grey, black and white. The female is a dark brown with light feather edges. The wings are grey-brown or green-brown with white tips. The bill is dark olive-grey with a black spot at the base.

19.

Goldeneye

Native to
Canada and
north-east America

Description

The Goldeneye is named after its striking eye colour and is another ancient breed. Fossil evidence leads experts to believe that the Goldeneye was around some 500,000 years ago.

In the late 1990s up to 400 Goldeneyes would spend the summer in the British Isles and up to 25,000 individuals would winter here. There is now a colony living in the Speyside area which is, without a doubt, due to the efforts of many enthusiasts who have provided nest boxes. The Goldeneye also nests in holes in trees left by woodpeckers. Nesting in trees is not without its dangers; the pine marten is always after an easy meal and is partial to eggs. However, The Boat of Garten Wildlife Group have come up with a cunning plan. They have mounted nest boxes on the top of shiny plastic pipes with great success. The pine martens cannot climb the pipe. The ducks must like them because one box contained sixteen eggs when the normal clutch is five to thirteen. The eggs are pale green, bluish or greyish.

Colour

The male's under-body, neck and breast are white. The upper-body is black and white with stripes on the sides. The head is a glossy green-black with a white oval between the eye and bill. The female has a brown head and her back, wings and tail are slate grey. The under-body, sides, breast and neck-band are white. Both males and females have yellow legs and eyes and black bills.

Harlequin

Native to
North America, Greenland, Iceland and Western Russia

Description

The Harlequin takes its name from the Italian character 'Arlecchino', a flamboyant comedy character dressed in bright clothes and a mask. In America the breed is also known as Lords and Ladies.

The Harlequin is truly an ancient breed. Remains found in Oregon, America have been identified as a Harlequin-type duck and the deposits in which they were found are around 23 million years old.

This fast-moving bird is at home by clear rushing water where it breeds, or by coastal rock pools and crashing surf in winter. They feed by diving for small insects and molluscs. The Harlequin's feathers are packed closely together to insulate it from the cold.

Harlequin nests are lined with down and are usually concealed in vegetation or natural hollows near fast-running streams. The Harlequin lays between five and ten creamy-yellow to pale buff eggs. The male stays until the ducklings are swimming about and occasionally the female will carry the young on her back.

Colour

The male has a bluish-grey body and chestnut sides. Black, white and chestnut lines run from the bill over the head to the base of the neck. There is a white spot on the cheek and several white lines near the front of the body. The wings have white and glossy-blue feathers. The tail is black. Females are brownish-grey with a white markings on the face. Both have brown eyes and bluish-grey legs, feet and bills.

Indian Runner

Black

Native to
The Far East, Indochina and Java

Description

The Indian Runner duck has been described by one expert as a 'bowling pin with legs and a beak' and was initially known to early sailors as the Penguin Duck. They were introduced into Europe in the early 19th century when a sea captain brought some ashore at Whitehaven in Cumbria.

This busy, busy duck, as its name suggests, runs everywhere searching the grass and meadows for tasty morsels such as slugs or snails. The Indian Runner duck is one of the best forms of organic pest control and this was their original use in the Far East where they were used to keep the rice fields free of nasties. Some western farmers are now breeding the Indian Runner for this purpose.

This is a dual-purpose breed that lays up to 200 eggs a year which vary between white, off-white and pale green. They seldom build nests, preferring to lay their eggs wherever they happen to be. They cannot fly. The females quack and the males have a hoarse whisper.

Colour

Males and females look much the same. The body and wings are black with a beetle-green lustre. The body under the wing is dark grey. The bill, legs are feet are dark grey and the eyes are dark brown. The drake's legs turn orange with age. Other colours include: fawn; fawn and white; chocolate; Cumberland blue; American fawn and white; penciled; mallard; trout; and white.

22.

Magpie
Blue and White

Native to
The British Isles

Description

The Magpie duck was developed by Oliver Drake and M C Gower-Williams in Wales in 1918 and 1919 by selectively breeding the Belgian Huttengem. A number of experts believe that it includes a touch of Indian Runner since the shape and carriage are so reminiscent of this breed.

The Magpie was bred as a dual-purpose breed and for exhibition. It is a difficult duck to breed to exhibition standard, so difficult that in 1998 the American Standards of Perfection eased the standard required. As a result of these difficulties the popularity of the Magpie duck never achieved the level it so justly deserved. A number of Magpie ducks were imported from America in the 1970s which gave the breed a boost in Britain and breeding numbers are increasing.

They are hardy ducks and active foragers or, as one breeder put it, garden wreckers. Slugs and snails are their favourites. Magpies are as happy on land as they are in water, they live for up to ten years and lay between 220 and 290 large green-blue eggs a year.

Colour

The male is blue and white with the blue mainly on the top of the head and the back. The legs, feet and bill are orange but the bill turns green with age. Other colours include: black and white; chocolate and white; and dun and white.

23.

Mallard

Native to
Most continents

Description

The Mallard is possibly the most well-known duck in the world. Records of this 'common' duck date back to the 8th century. There are 127,000 breeding pairs in the UK and 371,000 pairs winter here. Mallards can take off vertically and rise almost 11 metres with one flap of their powerful wings. Once in flight they can attain speeds of 21 metres a second.

The ducks pair in autumn but do not breed until the following spring. The nest is made up of twigs and grass and lined with down. It is built near calm, shallow water such as wetlands, rivers and streams and it could be on the ground hidden by dense vegetation or 12 metres up in a tree cavity. The nest is usually built by the female alone near to where she herself was hatched. The clutch of four to eighteen light greyish-green, buff or white eggs are laid at one a day. It is only after the last egg is laid that incubation begins and the male leaves. The ducklings are capable of feeding and swimming straight after hatching.

Colour

Males have an iridescent green head and upper neck, a white collar and a purple-brown breast. The upper-body is a brownish-grey and the under-body and sides are pale-grey. The wings are brownish-grey with white tips and some glossy blue feathers. The tail is black and curled. The bill is yellow to olive green and the eyes are brown. Females are mottled brown with a pinkish-brown bill and brown eyes. Both have orange legs.

24.

Mandarin

Native to
China

Description

After their first mating season the male and female will search for each other and re-bond in following seasons. It is this devotion that has led to the Mandarin being used as a symbol of love and fidelity at Chinese weddings.

This magnificent looking duck was once to be found all over Asia but we are responsible for a drop in numbers within the wild population. The Mandarin prefers to nest in tree cavities in densely wooded areas near to shallow water but logging has destroyed large areas of its breeding ground. Hunters who cannot tell one duck from another can mistake them in flight and shoot them although I am told the meat of the Mandarin has an unpleasant taste and it is therefore not deliberately hunted for food. Today there are small feral populations around the British Isles.

The Mandarin lays a clutch of nine to twelve eggs and both male and female will guard the ducklings. Despite this care less than a half the young will survive for more than two weeks because of predators.

Colour

Males have a black crown with a long crest, chestnut cheeks and white over the eye. The breast is maroon with vertical stripes; the under-body is white with gold and black sides. The wings are mainly olive brown, green, black and blue. The bill is red, the eyes are dark brown and the legs are orange-yellow. Females have a grey head and neck and a brown back with mottled sides. The bill is yellowish-brown and the eyes are brown.

Muscovy

Black

Native to
America

Description

Muscovy refers to the area centring around Moscow although it is doubtful whether these ducks have ever seen Moscow, let alone lived there. In the 16th to 17th centuries the Company of Merchant Adventurers to New Lands traded ducks to Europe. At one time the company was known as the Muscovy or Muscovite Company and it is probable the name was attached to the ducks they traded. It is sometimes also known as the Barbary duck. The Muscovy was mentioned by Carl Linnaeus in 1758 and his description was to the point: 'a duck with a naked and carunculated [meaning having fleshy growths] face'.

Muscovys live by streams, lakes and forest swamps where their diet consists of vegetation grazed from the water, small fish, reptiles and insects. They build nests in hollows in trees and lay a clutch of between eight and ten white eggs a year. The male has a dry hissing call and the female a gentle trilling *coo*. The large numbers of wild Muscovy ducks are becoming a nuisance even in the south of England and steps are being taken to reduce the numbers.

Colour

Wild Muscovys are blackish while the majority of domesticated ones are dark brown or black and white. The wings have metallic green feathers and white patches. The female is similar colours but not as bright. Both males and females have yellow or grey-blue bills with a central black stripe. Their eyes are brown and their legs are grey. Other colours include: blue; chocolate; white; lavender; bronze; barred and ripple.

26

Orpington
Buff

Native to
The British Isles

Description

The original Orpingtons were blue and developed using the Cayuga, Indian Runner, Aylesbury and Rouen breeds. William Cook from the village of Orpington in Kent then used these blue Orpingtons to breed the buff variety at the end of the 19th century. Four other colours do exist but are rarely seen.

The Orpington was developed as a dual-purpose breed and lays in the region of 220 white or slightly tinted eggs a year, which is slightly more than the average duck. They are not a difficult breed to raise and are now mainly kept for purely ornamental purposes and live for eight to twelve years if foxes and other nasties do not intervene.

Like all domestic ducks they require protection from the wind and rain and a regular supply of fresh water. Their ability to fly is not great and so only a low fence is required to keep them at home.

Colour

Males and females are both buff coloured and the male has a glossy seal-brown head. The feet and legs are orange-yellow and the eyes are brown. The male's bill is yellow and the female's is brown-orange. Other Orpington colours include: blue; white; black and brown.

27

Pekin

Native to
China

Description

The Pekin duck developed from the Mallard on the waterways of Nanjing in China. They were exported to the British Isles and America in 1873 where they are also known as the Long Island duck. This is a heavy duck, weighing up to 5kg, which stands almost vertically with a walk similar to a penguin. Because of their weight, flight is not common.

The Pekin is a highly intelligent breed and can become a loyal pet. It appears that, on occasion, they prefer human company to that of other ducks. The life span of a Pekin duck, if not struck down by the vagaries of nature and predators, is between nine and twelve years and they will lay an average of 200 eggs a year in an area which they feel is safe.

Unless ducklings are reared naturally, by a genuine duck, when they enter water they will sink. The mother ensures her ducklings are adequately waterproofed but incubator-raised ducklings do not have this protection. A pond full of sinking fluffy yellow ducks is not a pretty sight.

Colour

They are white with a yellow tinge.
The legs and bill are deep orange

28

Pintail

Native to
Northern Europe

Description

There is fossil evidence that suggests the Pintail's ancestors were dabbling in the ponds of the British Isles 500,000 years ago. A skeleton of a Pintail was also found at almost 5,000 metres on the south slopes of Mount Everest.

The population of the Pintail is governed by many factors from disease to the problems of hunting, fishing and by wetlands and grassland being converted to farmland – early planting means the Pintail's nests are destroyed. Despite these setbacks the numbers have not significantly decreased. The Pintail is considered a 'quarry' species meaning it can legally be shot in winter. The sheer speed at which the Pintail flies and its aerial agility make it a challenge for the hunter. It is suggested that the numbers hunted each year should be restricted.

The Pintail lays between six to twelve greenish or cream eggs a year. Their nests are built from dry vegetation, hidden in other vegetation and lined with feathers and down. The male's call is a *proop-proop* whistle and the female a quack or a croak.

Colour

The male's head is brown. The breast and front of the neck are white with stripes each side of the neck. The upper-body and sides are speckled grey and the rump has a white patch on each side. The two long tail feathers are black and the others are grey outlined in white. The legs and bill are shades of grey and the eyes are yellow-brown. The female is a mottled brown and has a shorter tail than the male.

29.

Red-Billed Pintail

Native to
Madagascar and east and southern Africa

Description

The Red-Billed Pintail or, in Afrikaans, the *Rooibekeend*, is the most common duck in South Africa. When there is sufficient food and water the Red-Billed Pintail is a home bird but in the dry season they will fly up to 1,100 miles to find suitable wetlands, shallow lakes, ponds and streams with ample food and floating vegetation. Their diet is mainly aquatic plants, grain, seeds, and insects but their bill is also adapted to catch shrimps, crabs and fish.

The breeding pair stay together for a long time and some experts say for life. The nest is built entirely by the female in a ground hollow of leaves and grass and lined with down. The clutch is usually five to twelve buff, cream or greenish-white eggs. The ducklings take to the water as soon as they are dry and are looked after by the female with the male hovering as guardian. Though they are hunted, the Red-Billed Pintail is not a threatened species. Their main threats are the African duck leech and the change or loss of nesting areas.

Colour

The male has a brown head and upper-body with buff-white feather edges that give a scalloped effect. The under-body is similar but paler. The throat is buff-white. The wing feathers are brown, tipped with buff and greenish-black at the base. The bill is pink with a dark tip, the eyes are brown and the legs and feet are dark grey. The female is similar but the colours are not as bright.

30

Red-Crested Pochard

Native to

The southern European mainland and southern and central Asia

Description

The Red-Crested Pochard is to be found mainly in Spain and Asia and as smaller numbers in France, Germany, the Netherlands and the south and east of the British Isles. It is thought that the British and Dutch flocks developed from escapees who bred in the wild to form a feral population. They are of the diving duck family and are to be found around lowland marshes and reed-fringed lakes. They build nests of roots, twigs and leaves amongst the lakeside vegetation and live mainly on grass, small plants and small aquatic life. They lay eight to twelve pale green eggs. The ducklings are flying by the time they are seven or eight weeks old and breed the following year.

Though they are not officially considered at risk, Red-Crested Pochards are threatened by loss of their nesting habitat, the lowering of water quality in wetlands leading to a loss of diet and unregulated hunting in France, Spain, Portugal and Iran.

The male has a round orange head, white flanks, a brown back and black breast and tail. The bill and eyes are reddish. The female is mainly pale brown with a darker back and crown and a whitish face. Her bill and eyes are a reddish-brown.

31

Redhead

Native to
Western North America

Description

There is no doubt how this duck got its name. Although the Redhead is a North American breed it is becoming more frequently spotted in Europe and there were several sightings in the British Isles in 2008.

The Redhead is mainly vegetarian but in the summer it will eat small aquatic insects and grasshoppers. When it does decide to build a nest the Redhead builds it of grass and other vegetation near freshwater lakes, marshes, swamps and rivers. Normally it prefers not to build a nest but rather 'borrows' one from a gull or other duck species where it lays its seven or eight white, pale-buff or greenish eggs. The eggs are laid over a period of days and after the second egg is laid the female will line the nest with her own feathers. After breeding, the male abandons the female and heads towards another large area of water where it moults and for a month is unable to fly. The male's call is a deep meow or purr while the females quack or squawk. A duck that purrs? Unbelievable but true.

Colour

The male's head and neck are chestnut red. The sides are a pale spotted grey and the upper-body and back are a darker spotted grey. The under-body is pale grey shading to white. The breast, tail, neck and rump are black and they have a blue bill. The female is brown and has a dark blue bill with a black tip. The males and females both have yellow eyes and grey legs.

32.

Ringed Teal

Native to
South America

Description

The Ringed Teal lives in South America and is one of the smallest ducks at only 30 to 38 cm long and weighing only 300 grams but they are fast and nimble and what they lack in size they make up for in style. To impress a female the male will swim around her in a figure of eight while throwing his head back and whistling. Many ducks breeds lose their plumage after mating and, for a time, look dowdy. The Ringed Teal looks good all year round.

Ringed Teal pairs bond for a considerable time, if not for life. Their nests are usually built in a natural hollow in a high tree and they have long, sharp claws which make perching in trees much easier and safer. They lay a clutch of five to twelve whitish eggs and the male helps to care for the brood. The duckling's feathers are waterproof before they leave the nest. The mother calls to them from the ground and the young throw themselves from the nest, bouncing on the ground or landing in the water with a splash. Injuries are very rare.

Colour

The male has a fawn-coloured head with a black line from the top of the head to the base of the neck. The back is chestnut and the sides are pale grey. The breast is black-speckled salmon pink. The bill is bluish-grey and the eyes are brown. The female has an olive-brown back and white blotches on the head. The feathers on the breast and under-body have a barred pattern. Both have iridescent green feathers mainly on the wings, a pale rump and a black tail.

33

Rosy-Billed Pochard

Native to
South America

Description

Rosy-Billed Pochards are frequently simply called Rosybills and are found in Brazil, Chile and Argentina, sometimes at altitudes of 3,000 metres.

This friendly duck will live peacefully alongside other breeds although if kept with Red-Crested Pochard, White-Faced Whistling or Carolina ducks it will successfully produce little hybrid ducklings. With all other breeds, given sufficient personal territory, peace and harmony are the order of the day.

Rosy-Billed Pochards breed well in captivity, happily nesting on the ground if there is sufficient vegetation or, failing that, in a good quality nesting box. They are winter hardy but must be provided with shelter and deep water where they can dive. They will occasionally spend the night on the water. Their preferred foods are seeds, roots and the leaves of aquatic plants.

Colour

The male is glossy purple-black with grey sides and a white area under the tail. The bill is bright red with a red knob at the base. The eyes are red and the legs are yellow-orange. The female is mainly brown with white under the tail and, on occasion, has brown eyes. The female's face may whiten with age.

34

Rouen

Native to
France

Description

The Rouen, pronounced Roan and also known as the Rouen Foncé was developed in France but it was not until the early 19th century when it arrived in the British Isles that it was improved to the high standard of quality and appearance for which it is known today. The Rouen (or Rhone as it was at the time) was one of the first ducks to be standardised in the British Isles, in 1865. In 1850 the Rouen arrived in America where it was used as a general farm duck.

The Rouen was bred originally for meat but is now mainly a decorative breed. Their egg production is not one of the best at only about 50-125 whitish eggs a year. The Rouen is very similar in appearance to a Mallard but is a much larger bird and brighter in colour. I understand that blue and apricot versions have been bred in Germany.

Colour

The male has a rich green-and-purple head with a white ring around the base of the neck which is not joined at the back. The breast is a rich purplish-brown, the under-body is a soft grey and the wings are brown and grey with a greenish-purple ribbon across them. The tail is dark brown-black. The bill is yellow with a green tint and a black spot at the tip. The female is mahogany brown with greenish-black or brown stripes across the feathers

35

Ruddy Shelduck

Native to
Spain, south-east Asia, Mongolia, north-west Africa and the Ethiopian highlands

Description

The Ruddy Shelduck has not yet become established as a feral breeding group in the British Isles but flocks have been seen regularly in Norfolk. Feral groups can be seen across northern Europe from Iceland to Maderia.

Treatment of the Ruddy Shelduck varys greatly from country to country. In Switzerland it has become a major problem. In 2004 420 were seen on the Klingnau dam and, because they are aggressive to other waterfowl, measures have been put in place to protect the local birds. In Tibet, Mongolia and other Buddhist countries the Ruddy Shelduck is considered sacred because their colour resembles that of a monk's robes. In Iran they are hunted for sport and commerce.

The Ruddy Shelduck will nest in open country in hollows, abandoned burrows, crevices in rocks and cliffs or hollows in tree trunks and will lay up to twelve creamy-white eggs.

They are aggressive in captivity unless they have plenty of space.

Colour

The male has a chestnut body. The head and neck are buff coloured and in the mating season there is a black ring at the base of the neck. The tail and rump are black. The female has no neck ring and has white on the face. The bills of both the males and females are black as are the legs and feet. The eyes are dark brown.

36

Saxony

Native to
Germany

Description

The Saxony was developed in the 1930s in the East German city of Chemnitz by crossing the Blue Pomeranian, the German Pekin and the Rouen. The breed was unveiled to the public at the Saxony Show in 1934 from which it subsequently took its name. Unfortunately, the breeding population of Saxony ducks was almost wiped out during World War II. Albert Franz started again but it was not until 1982 that it was officially recognised in the British Isles. Even today there are few breeders and little is written about these beautiful ducks.

The breed arrived in America in 1984. Holderread Waterfowl Farm imported these and are one of the largest breeders of the Saxony in America. Sadly the breed is still considered critical.

The number of eggs laid seems to vary quite widely from 100 to 240 white to grey-white eggs a year. The Saxony are placid, child-friendly and noisy pets. They will keep your garden clear of slugs and snails but will also clear it of cabbages, cauliflowers and lettuce.

Colour

The male's head and neck are silver blue-grey with a white ring. The under-body and sides are cream and they have a burgundy-chestnut breast. The bill is yellow or orange, sometimes with pale green shading. The females are buff coloured with white face stripes and neck ring. The bill is orange, sometimes with brown shading. The legs and feet of all Saxonys are orange to reddish-orange and the eyes are dark brown.

37

Sharp-Winged Teal

Native to

The highlands of central Peru, northern Chile and Argentina

The Sharp Winged Teal is also known as the Speckled Teal and originates in the highlands of central Peru. There are sub-species which cover most of South America and out to the Falkland Islands.

In the wild they tend to gather in groups of about 20 birds but the flock sizes increase outside the mating season. The birds usually pair for a year and lay in the region of five to eight creamy-white eggs which the male helps to raise. What happens to the pair after that year is unclear.

The average size of the Sharp Winged Teal is around 38 to 45 cm in length. They are generally said to be winter hardy and are content in captivity provided they have shelter and an ice-free pond. This is not an aggressive bird and will live quite happily among other breeds. This duck does not quack but rather goes *preep-preep*.

Colour

The males's upper-body is brownish with speckles. The head and neck are greyish-fawn with fine black speckles. The under-body and breast are pinkish-grey with highly visible brown spots. The wings are brown with metallic-green secondary feathers. The beak is usually blue-grey, the eyes are brown and the legs are grey. The female is similar but the colours are duller.

38

Silky

Native to
America

Description

The Silky as we know it today was originated and developed by Darrell Sheraw of Pennsylvania, USA. The white variety was first on the pond followed by black, snowy and grey. These delightful little birds tend to be lighter than other duck breeds.

Drawings and paintings suggest that crested ducks have been around for 2,000 years and the crested domestic duck arrived on the scene in the 1600s. There are some people who believe that the Silky made its first appearance in the British Isles but while this is commonly considered unlikely, it was definitely first exhibited here and is mentioned in several early poultry books.

Silkys make excellent mothers and take great care of their offspring until they are safe from predators. They are unable to fly and so make ideal pets. They are good at foraging and apart from the molluscs and snails that they find in the pond they are partial to a handful of grain.

Colour

They are black with silky, soft feathering. The head is green and some have a black crest the size of a golf ball.

39

Silver Appleyard

Native to
The British Isles

Description

The Silver Appleyard was developed by Reginald Appleyard, a renowned breeder of waterfowl, at his Priory Waterfowl Farm in West Suffolk in the 1940s. His wish was to develop a duck which would be the best of all worlds: producing good quality meat while laying 100 to 180 large white eggs a year as well as being good looking and the ideal ornamental addition to any group. Through his expertise and hard work his wish was granted and the Silver Appleyard is known worldwide as an 'ideal duck'.

To achieve this feathered masterpiece Reginald Appleyard crossed the large breeds, Rouen, Aylesbury and Pekin. There is also a miniature version of the Silver Appleyard which was developed by Tom Bartlett in the 1970s and 80s.

The Silver Appleyard makes an ideal pet because of its calm and docile temperament but please do not keep a single duck. A single duck is an unhappy duck so you must keep a minimum of two in order for them to lead a happy and healthy life. They, like you, need friends and companions.

Colour

The male has a beetle-green head and neck and a white throat with fawn markings. The breast, wings, tip of the tail and the ring around the neck are silver-white. The wings are grey and white with a blue stripe. The female is silver-white with large amounts of fawn flecks on back. Both males and females have yellow bills, orange legs and feet and dark hazel eyes.

40

South African Shelduck

Native to
South Africa

Description

The South African or Cape Shelduck can now be found in Zimbabwe, Zambia, Namibia and Botswana. In the winter they tend to migrate to the north-east and congregate in large flocks where they go through a moulting period during which they cannot fly. It is generally believed that once the male and female bond they stay together for life. The breeding area is usually in open country where there is access to lakes and rivers.

The South African Shelduck nests on hillsides, usually in holes abandoned by other animals. Deep burrows help to protect the birds from the high temperatures to be found in their breeding areas. Their favourites are those made by aardvarks or porcupines.

During the breeding season the ducks become vegetarian and feed on grain, seedlings, seeds, peanuts and figs; the rest of the time they eat small shellfish, shrimps, crayfish and possibly small crabs. They lay ten to fifteen creamy coloured eggs and the ducklings are protected by both parents.

Colour

The male has a grey head and upper neck. The lower neck and breast are pale chestnut and the rest of the body is chestnut red. The tail is black. The female is slightly darker with a white patch around the eyes. Both the males and females have black bills, legs and feet. Their eyes are brown.

41.

Swedish Blue

Native to
Sweden

Description

The Swedish Blue was first seen in the British Isles in the mid 19th century but had been strutting its stuff in Europe for quite some time before this. In Europe they went by the name of Swedish or Pommern after the region of Pomerania which was part of Sweden at the time and where the farmers had been raising this attractive bird since the early 19th century.

It was believed that their colour gave them a certain amount of protection from four-legged predators as they blended with the background. There is only one colour which is considered standard: blue. I am told that the black is actually a blue that hasn't bred true or, as they used to say in the textile trade, it's a bad black.

Swedish Blues are hardy and produce superb-tasting meat. It is a slow-maturing breed and this possibly accounts for their excellent flavour. They lay between 100 and 150 green or blue-tinted eggs a year. They are calm and easy going so make good pets. However, they do not like being confined so freedom in an orchard or a paddock is ideal.

Colour

The male is a bluish slate grey with a white patch from the front of the neck to the breast. He has a dark blue head with a greenish bill and bright brown eyes. The legs are also brown. The female is the same as the male except that the head matches the body. Occasionally on both there will be two or three white wing feathers.

42

Tufted

Native to
The British Isles, Europe, Iceland, America and Alaska

Description

The Tufted duck can be found in most lowland areas of the British Isles and possibly the greatest numbers are to be found around Norwich. This is a duck with a population of around one million birds; please don't ask me how they count them! In the British Isles alone there are up to 8,000 breeding pairs so the odds of seeing a Tufted duck are pretty good. They tend to congregate around lakes, ponds and gravel pits where they feed on vegetation, insects and freshwater mussels.

Their nests are usually built in the thick vegetation on the shore of a lake or pond. Small islands are their preference. The nests are built by the females and are either isolated or loosely grouped with other Tufted ducks' nests. They lay in the region of six to fourteen olive, grey or greenish eggs.

The main threats to the Tufted are hunting and egg collecting in Iceland, chemical and noise pollution, land drainage, the increase in the use of waterways for recreation and the American mink which is a ruthless predator brought to the British Isles in 1929.

Colour

The male has a glossy black head with a trailing crest. The upper-body is black and the sides and under-body are white. The bill is grey-blue with a light grey central line and tip. The eyes are yellow. The female has a dark brown head and a short crest. The upper-body is varying shades of brown and the under-body and sides are shades of white.

43

Welsh Harlequin

Native to
The British Isles, Europe and America

Description

The Welsh Harlequin was originally developed by Group Captain Leslie Bonnet in 1949. Group Captain Bonnet discovered a rare but attractive colour mutation in his flock of khaki Campbells which he selectively bred to form the basis of what was to become the Welsh Harlequin.

In the late 1960s the breed was almost extinct but Edward Grayson of Lancaster came to the rescue. He had kept ducks from the original Bonnet strain and with careful selection to stabilise the colour he secured the future of the Welsh Harlequin. In 1968 the first Harlequin eggs were exported to Tennessee, America but by 1980 there were only two small flocks in the USA and the breed is now classed as critical.

This attractive dual-purpose duck is considered ideal for the back garden. It is a good forager and not a great flyer. A Welsh Harlequin will lay in the region of 250-300 white to greenish eggs a year. Should be enough for a couple of omelettes.

Colour

The male's head is greenish-black and there is a white ring around the neck. The shoulders are claret fringed with white and the breast is creamy claret. The upper back has a tortoise shell appearance of white and brown. The rump is dark brown or bronze. The bill is olive green with a black tip, the legs and feet are orange and the eyes are brown to cinnamon. The female is shades of brown and cream with occasional speckles.

44

White-Faced Whistling

Native to

South America and Africa

Description

The White-Faced Whistling is found in South America especially Panama and Costa Rica, in South Africa south of the Sahara desert and in Madagascar and the Comoro Islands.

I am told it is an impressive sight to see a flock of 1,000 White-Faced Whistling ducks flying over head at dawn calling to one and other.

The White Faced Whistling mates for life which could be fifteen years. They build their nest of sticks on the ground in an area covered by vegetation or they occasionally nest in trees. The clutch is usually between eight and fourteen creamy white eggs. They spend the days on the banks of pools and rivers preening themselves and the evenings on the water feeding.

Their white faces and their triple whee-whee-whee call make them one of the easier birds to identify. The call is made to keep in contact with other White-Faced Whistling ducks. There are nine other species of whistling duck, each with its own inimitable call.

Colour

The face is white to just behind the eyes, like a mask. The throat is also white. The back of the head and upper neck is black changing to chestnut lower down. The top of the breast is also chestnut. The upper-body is brown with fawn-edged feathers and the wings are brown. The bill is long and bluish-grey as are the longish legs. The eyes are dark brown. The female is similar in appearance but not as bold.

Duck Talk

Drake – An adult male duck

Hen – An adult female duck (sometimes simply called a duck)

Duckling – A young duck still in downy plumage

Brood – A group of ducklings

Clutch – The eggs produced in one batch

Bantam – A small duck breed

Crest – A tuft of feathers on the back of the head

Preen – To clean and re-arrange feathers using the bill

Down – A layer of fine feathers under the tougher exterior ones

Self-sustaining – A flock which will grow and develop without needing outside input

Feral – A duck which was once domesticated but which has escaped or been released and returned to the wild

Dual-purpose – A breed used to produce both meat and eggs

Spectacles – A term coined by the author to describe pale rings around the eyes

Collective terms for ducks

There are a number of terms used for a group of ducks. A group on water may be referred to as a **raft**, a **paddling** or a **bunch**. A when they are in flight they may be called a **team**, a **flight** or a **flock**. Many other terms are dependent upon the breed of duck, for example, a group of Mallards on land is called a **sord**. Two ducks together is a **brace**.

About the Author

Jack Byard was born in Bradford in Yorkshire where he has lived and worked all of his life. A Rolls Royce mechanic by trade and a jewellery craftsman in later years, Jack spent the latter part of his working life imparting this knowledge as a school workshop technician.

Jack has always had a deep affection for his rural heritage and so wrote his first book, *Know Your Sheep*, with a view to sharing with others the countryside that he loves. Three years later and there is no sign of a quiet retirement for Jack just yet. *Know Your Ducks* is his eigth *Know Your…* title.

Also in the 'Know Your' series...

Know Your Sheep
Forty-one breeds of sheep which can be seen on Britain's farms today.

Know Your Tractors
Forty-one tractors working today including classics and modern machines.

Know Your Cattle
Forty-four breeds of cattle. Some you will recognise and some are rare.

Know More Sheep
A further forty-four sheep breeds including popular mules and a few unfamiliar faces.

Know Your Combines
Forty-three combines you are likely to see in the summertime fields.

Know Your Horses
Forty-three breeds living around Britain today and a few rare ponies.

Know Your Pigs
Twenty-eight breeds of pig in every shape and size. Some you will know, and some you won't.

Know Your Trucks
Forty-four example of trucks that you are likely to see driving Britain's roads today.

Know Your Chickens
A colourful selection of forty-four chickens in every shape, size and colour.

Know Your Buses
Forty-four models of bus out and about on the roads of Britain today.

Know Your Donkeys
Forty-four breeds from miniature to mammoth with a few mules thrown in